SOUTH WALES RAILWAYS AROUND THE MILLENNIUM

Paul Woollard

AMBERLEY

Front cover: On the sad occasion of the last ever working of a train from Cwm-mawr to Coedbach, cut-down No. 08994 approaches the village of Pontyberem with its train of prime Welsh anthracite coal. This line, part of a small network built by the Burry Port & Gwendraeth Railway, used the course of a canal to reach the important mining area at the head of the Gwendraeth Valley. The alignment retained the canal's over bridges, necessitating the use of reduced clearance locomotives and, where appropriate, rolling stock. 29 March 1996.

Rear cover: With the kind permission of Taylor Woodrow Mining, the Author was able to obtain this view at the Cwmbargoed Disposal Point loading pad where, headed by Nos 37897 and 37797, the 7C34 to Aberthaw Power Station was being loaded. With the inevitable deposit of coal dust on the running rails, it was perhaps unsurprising that the train ran on a short distance after each brake application as the consist was moved through the loading pad! 14 April 1995.

First published 2019

Amberley Publishing
The Hill, Stroud
Gloucestershire, GL5 4EP

www.amberley-books.com

Copyright © Paul Woollard, 2019

The right of Paul Woollard to be identified as the Author of this work has been asserted in accordance with the Copyrights, Designs and Patents Act 1988.

ISBN 978 1 4456 8900 5 (print)
ISBN 978 1 4456 8901 2 (ebook)

All rights reserved. No part of this book may be reprinted or reproduced or utilised in any form or by any electronic, mechanical or other means, now known or hereafter invented, including photocopying and recording, or in any information storage or retrieval system, without the permission in writing from the Publishers.

British Library Cataloguing in Publication Data.
A catalogue record for this book is available from the British Library.

Origination by Amberley Publishing.
Printed in the UK.

Introduction

A gloriously sunny, if a little misty, Sunday morning in October 1995 found me at the head of the Taff Bargoed Valley waiting patiently for an Aberthaw to Cwmbargoed empty MGR. The waiting was no hardship in the still peace, with little bar the distant sound of birds of prey to disturb the rugged, mountainous scenery. After a while, a distant rumble could be made out further down the valley, rising in volume for several minutes until the distinctive noise of two hardworking Class 37s could be discerned from the noise. For a further ten minutes this sound increased in volume and clarity until the curvy 'glint' from the roofs of two distant locomotives could be made out, followed by the dull shapes of hoppers moving against the landscape. Ever closer, the thunderous roar of two English Electric 12SVT engines reached a crescendo as the glinting form of the train dominated my camera frame. The moment was recorded at a 250th of a second, just as the engines throttled back, their distinctive turbo 'spool down' giving way to the 'clack-clack clack-clack' of thirty-odd empty MGR hoppers moving towards their destination of Cwmbargoed Disposal Point. I walked away thinking I'd just witnessed something very special, perhaps unique to South Wales – a feeling that has not diminished in nearly twenty-four years!

A native of rural Gloucestershire, I grew up in the Berkeley Vale, initially at Purton, near the banks of the River Severn. My earliest association with railways involved glimpsing trains across the river, and being the proud owner of a Hornby trainset at the age of ten. A few years later, fascinated by a chance encounter with a Class 25 shunting at Bristol Parkway, I became deeply enthusiastic about the railway scene of the late 1970s. Trips with my father, a Severn river pilot, involving rail journeys either to or from Barry, on the Vale of Glamorgan, to pick up or alight from ships fuelled this enthusiasm. My lasting impressions from these late 1970s childhood trips into South Wales was of a veritable kaleidoscope of images, starting as our train sped westward from the Severn Tunnel past lines of sooty-roofed 'corporate' blue locos stabled next to the yards at Severn Tunnel Junction. With my Ian Allan *ABC* at hand, frantic scribbling accompanied the sight of more work-stained blue motive power, together with lines of rust-coloured wagons as Newport East Usk, ADJ and Ebbw Junction sped by. From the gentle, curving eastward approach to Cardiff, the rust-red remains of East Moors Steelworks dominating the skyline gave way to more lines of wagons, punctuated by locos, as Cardiff Central was approached. Here, platforms dominated by smoking, rattling DMUs often echoed to the roof-raising sound of through freights hauled by more grimy blue Class 37s. As our DMU from Cardiff approached Barry, the weed-covered sidings and surviving coal hoists provided fascinating clues to a long-gone prosperous past... I was hooked!

It was to be nearly fifteen years before I returned to South Wales, armed with my camera, to try and record some of what had left such an impression on me as a child. Before looking at what I was to encounter in the early 1990s, it is perhaps appropriate to briefly look at the history of the rail network in that area.

By the early years of the twentieth century, the development of rail transport in South Wales had produced an intricate and massively complicated network that owed its origins to several factors that came into play in the previous century. Firstly, the ironmasters of north Monmouthshire and Glamorgan who, by the middle of the nineteenth century, were well established at locations where iron ore, limestone and coal – essential ingredients for the production of pig iron – needed a way of transporting their products to ports for onward shipment. Works at Blaenavon, Ebbw Vale and Dowlais – the latter run by the biggest iron company in the world in 1839 – were instrumental in railways superseding canals as the primary mode of transport in that area. The demand for high-quality Welsh anthracite coal in the second half of the nineteenth century saw an immense development of rail transport, chiefly in the South Wales Valleys, that connected with the great ports of Newport, Cardiff and Swansea – themselves undergoing considerable expansion to cope with the new traffic. Concurrent with this was the westward expansion of the South Wales Railway, linking Gloucester with Cardiff, Swansea and Carmarthen by 1852. Add to this the later nineteenth-century development of new ports at Penarth and Barry, the latter an integrated rail and port company – the Barry Railway – and some idea of the growing network can be imagined. An indication of this is the fact that Merthyr and Dowlais were served by no less than six railway companies at the beginning of the twentieth century!

Besides coal and iron, chemicals and tinplate influenced railway construction, especially in the Swansea area, over the same period. By the early twentieth century steel had replaced iron, with exhausted inland ore deposits giving rise to coastal plants at Port Talbot and Cardiff, and rail-hauled ore supplies up the valleys to the remaining works at the Heads of the Valleys, such as Ebbw Vale and Dowlais. The aforementioned massive demand for Welsh coal reached its peak in 1913 with 56 million tons – 20 per cent of UK production – being exported. From here on, however, a gradual decline set in for the demand in locally mined coal, not least due to the rise in the use of oil but also more demanding geological conditions affected extraction costs.

Despite new industries like petrochemicals in the Swansea area, and the continued importance of general industry in South Wales, together with Fishguard being developed as a port, the GWR began to cut back the overcomplicated network of railways in the 1920s. Roughly in parallel with the decline in coal mining, the network steadily contracted over the next sixty years, with the devastating miners' strike of 1984/85 steepening the decline in traffic and network mileage. Though core passenger services remained, together with modern steel plants providing traffic to and from the likes of Llanwern, Port Talbot, Tremorfa and Ebbw Vale Tinplate Works, the South Wales railway scene of the 1990s was a shadow of its former self. However, set against this, coal was still a significant source of traffic, with flows from Cwmbargoed and Cwmgwrach, at the head of the Taff Bargoed and Neath valleys, respectively, to the large power station at Aberthaw, as well as to local coastal steelworks.

It was this much contracted railway network that I began to explore in the 1990s, with the inevitable feeling that myself and other photographers were picking over what was left of a once great industrial system. The passing of the last deep mines and, as the years went by, more of the South Wales steel industry, together with petrochemical plants, seemed to reinforce this view. With decline, however, came the chance to record the sheer variety and colour of some of the railborne traffic that could still be found in the area at the time of the new millennium, in landscapes that could be both beautiful and heavily industrialised. With reference to the opening paragraph to this introduction, the sheer impact of the remaining 'classic' diesel types, like the venerable Class 37, seemed inseparable from these scenes – something that was to act as a repeated draw to many – even as the twenty-first century saw such types gradually fade away. It is with the above in mind that the contents of this collection evolved, combining colour, landscapes and motive power variety.

Images collected over such a relatively short period, into which factors the weather, actual running of a service and, not least, things like one's own work have to be considered, inevitably mean many lines are covered on the same date. Here I hope the images make up for this duplication on any given day. Also, over what now really does seem like a very short period of time, it is worth mentioning that a fair bit of this collection could not have been gained without the help of others. These people take the form of friends in whose company I re-learned the importance of sacrificing lineside time for investigative groundwork and, significantly, the wonderfully helpful reliefs at some of the remaining manual signalboxes in the area. A handful of coins and a knowledge of local phone boxes from which to ring the signalmen contributed to significant results at a time just before mobile phones were commonplace!

What exploring the railways of South Wales did for me was to encourage a look at the history surrounding any given location visited. A hunt for reference material would always follow any photographic trip. This side of the interest has made it into many of the captions accompanying the images in this album, together with, where space allows, a brief look at the life of some of the motive power illustrated. I hope this adds to the enjoyment of the book, as well as possibly encouraging the reader to go out and do the same!

Finally, for ease of presentation, the images are arranged geographically in an east to west fashion, with the crude analogy of an 'upturned comb' being applied, with the coastal main lines forming the base and the inland running routes, such as valley branches, being the comb's teeth. This way I hope the reader can roughly keep track of the book's progress through this beautiful and distinctive area of the United Kingdom.

Paul Woollard
Nailsworth, Gloucestershire
2019

How better to start a collection of images on South Wales than by starting at the border with England! The River Wye at Chepstow, which forms a natural border between the two countries at this point, can just be seen below No. 60008 and the total consist of a short 6E30 Margam to Hartlepool steel coil train. The Fairfields engineering complex and the beached MV *Breckland* can be seen in the background. Fairfields evolved from a private Wye shipyard that was brought under government control as National Shipyard No. 1 towards the end of the First World War. 'Standard' type ships were produced at the facility which, in later years, assembled sections of the 1966 Severn Bridge prior to their being floated to site via the Wye. 19 August 2003.

Bulwark, just over the border into South Wales, is the setting for this view of No. 56070 heading a Saturday 6E37 Llanwern to Lackenby empty slab train. As well as the River Wye in flood tide, the 1966-built Severn Bridge can be seen in a view that, from 1919 to the early 1920s, would have included large shipyard cranes on the opposite bank, assembled as part of the National Shipyard No. 2 project, set out in response to the huge merchant shipping losses during the First World War. New from Doncaster in 1979, No. 56070 was cut up at TJ Thompson, Stockton, in 2011. 28 August 2003.

This view at Bulwark, looking towards Chepstow, shows a Saturday Westerleigh to Robeston empty fuel tank train, then coded as 6B28, head into Wales behind Loadhaul-liveried No. 60008. In the right-hand distance the aforementioned Fairfields complex, together with the bridge carrying the railway over the Wye, can be seen. New from Brush in December 1992, No. 60008 has carried the names *Moel Fammau*, *Gypsum Queen II* and *Sir William McAlpine* during its lifetime. The loco has been stored since 2010. 8 August 2006.

The subject of this view, taken from the Wye crossing section of the 1966 Severn Bridge, is the Monday/Wednesday/Friday 6V14 Hull to Baglan Bay vinegar tanks, unusually double-headed by Nos 37218 and 37015. Across the Wye the Beachley Peninsula can be seen, together with Oldbury-on-Severn Power Station – located on the east bank of the Severn, the course of which the Wye will shortly join. Of note is that that Beachley boasted a small power station too, built in the 1920s as part of the National Shipyard No. 2 project, being closed shortly thereafter when the unused complex was wound down. 22 September 1993.

The River Severn and the original road crossing, yet to receive its coat of white paint, form part of the backdrop for this view of No. 56032 heading 6V67 (Scunthorpe Entrance 'C' to Cardiff Tidal). The location was Portskewett, seen from a bridge carrying a lane to 'Black Rock', itself once the location of the west bank terminal of the pre-Severn Tunnel rail-served ferry. A Doncaster product from 1977, No. 56032 was stored at the time of writing. 22 September 1993.

Though of reasonably poor quality, this shot is included for its rarity value showing, as it does, a rare trip of military supplies from the former MOD base at Caerwent, east of Newport. The Caerwent complex was originally developed as a propellant factory for the Royal Navy, being located not far from the left-hand side of this view of the short train crossing the (then) M4. The identity of the Class 08 is unknown. By the 1990s propellant stocks were being literally 'torched' to effect disposal. On one occasion, I well remember glimpsing what looked like a large match striking, followed by a gently rising plume of white smoke, in the general direction of Caerwent. This was a highly unusual distraction as I drove west over the Severn Bridge! 1 June 1993.

Like all steelmaking plant, the 'heavy end' of the Llanwern site – now no longer a feature of this complex – always produced some dramatic visual effects. Adding to the visible impact of steelmaking in midwinter, the one-minute exposure accentuates No. 60034's visual contribution to the scene as its engine is started prior to it collecting the train of empty iron ore tipplers visible in the background. Opened in 1962, the works was noteworthy for, among other things, the first successful use of a computer to control the hot strip mill operation. The 'heavy end' was demolished in 2004. 30 December 1991.

No. 60029 leaves Llanwern Steelworks on the first stage of its journey to Port Talbot with a train of empty iron ore tipplers. Class 60s were the last commonly used haulage type for this train, other locos being pairs of Class 56s and the even more impressive treble-headed Class 37 workings, starting in the 1970s. Alas, No. 60029 was withdrawn in 2013 after just under twenty-three years of service. 27 October 1992.

A final look at Llanwern sees No. 37213 making short work of a single-wagon trip from the steelworks as it nears East Usk Yard, Newport. The recent snowfall gives a different feel to this well-known shot which, not least due to the telephoto lens, highlights what was to disappear from the Gwent skyline by 2004. New to Swansea Landore in January 1964 as D6913, this loco was to spend much of its time in Wales before its transfer to Immingham in 1986. The loco has since been cut up. 8 February 1996.

Providing a visual contrast to much of what I was recording in South Wales at the time, No. 45596 *Bahamas* catches the glint from low March sunlight as it heads past the Somerton district of Newport with 'The Welsh Marches Express'. This train ran between Crewe and Worcester. 26 March 1994.

A multi-storey car park offers this view across the River Usk towards the St Julians area of Newport, taking in the remains of Newport Castle to the right of the main railway route through the city. Towards the end of No. 60015's train of Port Talbot-bound empty iron ore tipplers, coded 6B52, the 'North and West' route can just be seen curving northwards at Maindee Junction. The loss of railborne traffic was considerable when steelmaking finished at Llanwern. 13 March 2001.

Crossing over to take the 'North and West' route at Maindee Junction, RES-liveried No. 47771 heads 6M90, the 11.30 Alexandra Dock Junction Yard to Bescot, over the River Usk, east of Newport station. This interesting but relatively short-lived working called at Pontrilas, north of Abergavenny, on its journey northwards. 19 November 1999.

The 6Z52 Chirk Kronospan to Teingrace and return provided a chance to see regular Class 56 haulage in Wales in the second decade of the twenty-first century. Here, the empty consist passes Ponthir en route to Devon to load its cargo of logs. Colas Rail's No. 56094 is doing the honours. 30 January 2013.

An interesting feature of the 2003 timetable was the extension of Fishguard loco-hauled services onward from Cardiff Central. Ostensibly a freight engine, No. 37886 proved to be a popular choice on this day, bringing photographers out along its route, including here at Ponthir, north-east of Newport. 30 August 2003.

The first three carriages of this Saturday 1Z37 to Fishguard Harbour, hauled by No. 37405, show evidence of enthusiasts enjoying this loco-hauled service that had originated at Hereford. Making a spirited departure from Abergavenny, the train is framed by the Brecons towards Pen-y-Fan and a fine lower quadrant signal bracket. 30 August 2003.

North of Abergavenny, the 'North and West' route closely follows the border between England and Wales. Part of the Welsh village of Llanvihangel, situated 5 miles north of Abergavenny, forms the backdrop to this view of a Saturday 17.44 Cardiff to Manchester Piccadilly charter, top and tailed by Nos 47841 and 47839. The Virgin Trains livery on the leading loco and train consist stand out in the low early evening light as the train heads northwards through lengthening shadows. 27 August 2005.

The 1M59 Bristol to Warrington mail vans, hauled by No. 67030, speed north past the village of Llanvihangel, making an audiovisual impact that lasted barely half a minute before tranquillity returned... Arguably, this brief intrusion was in stark contrast to the multitude of huge lorries that have taken this, and other mail traffic, off the rails. 28 March 2002.

On this particular Saturday in March 2002, the 08.33 Manchester Piccadilly to Cardiff was formed of No. 37421 and a rake of Mk 2 stock, the livery of which closely resembled the British Rail corporate blue and grey scheme of the 1960s, '70s and early '80s. Such a standout livery lent itself to recording the train in the landscape, in this case behind part of the village of Llanvihangel. Unlike most of the Class 37s that appear in this book, this engine did not start life in South Wales, being new to Sheffield Darnall in 1965. Not until 1980, as No. 37267, did the loco gravitate to Wales with an allocation to Swansea Landore. Following mid-1980s refurbishment to a Class 37/4, No. 37421's life was to take a further twist as, following withdrawal in 2009, preservation at the Pontypool & Blaenavon Railway was followed by reinstatement under Colas ownership. 2 March 2002.

In the valley between Pandy and Pontrilas, north of Abergavenny, the 'North and West' route vies for space with the A465 road and the River Monow. The course of the Monow marks, roughly, the border between England and Wales as it winds through picturesque farmland. Here, Nos 37669 and 37670 are seen hauling 6W32 (Craven Arms to Newport), a Network Rail-branded empty ballast working. This colourful train was possibly the last time the Author recorded Class 37s in Wales on what could be described as a traditional freight duty. 19 March 2006.

Just a few metres upstream along the Monow from the previous view, No. 37418 heads a train that was one of a welcome (if brief) series of loco-hauled services covering a shortage of diesel multiple units. Though taken at roughly the same time of year as the previous photo, early spring blossom and budding trees give a much more vivid impression of the season. Now preserved on the East Lancs Railway, this locomotive was new to Cardiff Canton as D6971 in March 1965. 28 March 2002.

This final view from the 'North and West' route should, strictly speaking, not be included in this collection as it was taken in England. However, Pontrilas is only half a mile into England and, significantly, most of the scenery is Welsh, including the distant Brecon Beacons. Here we see D1015 *Western Champion*, then repainted into the 'Golden Ochre' livery in which it entered service in January 1963. The loco, which had returned to main line service just over a year before, was working the Pathfinder Tours 1Z31 'North Wales and Snowdonia Excursion' – run for the employees of Mendip Rail, Foster Yeoman and Hanson. In the still conditions that prevailed, the discernible noise of signal wires and the 'clack' of lower quadrant signal arms was a fitting precursor to the sound of hard-working twin Maybach engines followed by the hollow roar of hauled stock! 5 May 2003.

The main line to Cardiff at Ebbw Junction is the setting for this view which shows – apart from No. 60047 waiting to depart Alexandra Dock Junction (ADJ) Yard with the 6B83 Ebbw Vale to Margam – a grimy No. 56061 hauling the 6B57 Llanwern to Port Talbot Grange steelworks coal empties. These coal trains finished with the demise of the 'Heavy End' of the Llanwern complex. 29 October 1997.

Park Junction, south-west of Newport, is the scene for this view of No. 37197 heading towards Ebbw Junction and ADJ Yard with a loaded ballast train from Machen Quarry. Alan, the relief from the junction signal box, can be seen recovering the single line token for the Machen Branch. This individual was a character and gentleman, always helpful – typical of his kind in South Wales. 8 May 1996.

No. 60062, one of the then regular Class 60s covering South Wales steel traffic at the time, can be seen accelerating away from Park Junction with 6B76, the 14.47 train from Margam to Ebbw Vale. Being nearly midsummer, the sun was high enough and round enough to enable this view, including the fine lower quadrant signal bracket, to be obtained. Just visible to the left of the frame is Park Junction Signal Box, with the famous Newport Transporter Bridge visible on the skyline. 18 June 1995.

A Saturday morning 6B83 empty steel coil train from Ebbw Vale Tinplate Works to Margam, hauled by No. 60015, can be seen approaching Risca. The footbridge vantage point afforded a view of the twisting course of the Ebbw Vale to Park Junction route at this point, together with the Parish Church of St Mary the Virgin. The loco is still in service with DB at the time of writing, in late 2018. 19 July 1997.

Crosskeys is the location for this view of another Saturday 6B83 morning coil empty to Margam, the traction being provided by No. 60036. This is now the location of a station, completed in 2008, which was built on the site of the former station closed in 1962. At the time of writing, Arriva Trains Wales provides services to Newport and Cardiff. Around five months later the loco was to lose its *Sgurr Na Ciche* nameplates. 15 February 1997.

Pathfinder Tours' 1Z41 Crewe to Ebbw Vale (and return) is seen passing Brynithel, near Aberbeeg, hauled by Nos 37886 and 37707. For the assembled photographers, this train provided the rare opportunity to record alternative traction to the Class 60s that dominated rail movements on the line at the time. 2 June 2001.

Looking over Aberbeeg, towards Llanhilleth, a train of coils for Ebbw Vale, hauled by No. 60047, can be seen catching the glint in the steep-sided valley through which the line runs at that point. As one that always considered he had arrived in South Wales too late to record what might be considered the archetypal 'industrial' Welsh valley scene, I felt that, with the mist and smoke from the small foundry, this image was a reminder of a bygone era that, for better or worse, had long passed. 29 October 1997.

Stood on the barren evidence of what was a far more extensive track layout at Aberbeeg, I recorded a Sunday 6B76 coil working from Margam, hauled by No. 60065, which had just passed No. 60069 on the 6B73 empty to Margam. Just visible, having overseen the crossing of trains, is Ralph – the signalman relief – seen returning to the signal box. At the invitation of this fine gentleman I saw the interior of Aberbeeg Signal Box. The frame consisted mainly of white (out of use) levers, alluding to the rationalised layout mentioned above. This was the site of a junction to a line that connected to the former 'Heads of the Valleys' line at Brynmawr, via Six Bells and Nantyglo. 4 June 1995.

Nearing the end of its outbound journey from Crewe to Ebbw Vale, Pathfinder Tours' 1Z41, hauled by Nos 37886 and 37707, passes the village of Cwm en route to run round in preparation for the return working. 2 June 2001.

Taken from the same footbridge as the previous view of 1Z41, though looking in the opposite direction, No. 56076 can be seen heading a lengthy Saturday 6B83 empty coil working to Margam past Cwm. This was the only sunny shot I managed of a Class 56 on the Ebbw Vale branch. Released from Doncaster in 1980, No. 56076 was withdrawn in 2008. 8 February 1997.

The sheer size of even part of the Ebbw Vale Tinplate Works can be seen in this view of a Sunday afternoon train leaving the complex behind No. 60059. Note the pair of Hunslet Barclay shunters at rest next to the welfare facility. Starting with the production of pig iron in 1790, the site developed into the largest steel mill in Europe by the late 1930s, employing the latest American production technology. Developed from 1974, roughly in parallel with the rundown of steel making on the site, the Tinplate Works seen here closed in July 2002, with the loss of 780 jobs. 22 June 2001.

Having taken the Machen Branch at Park Junction, Newport, a freshly repainted No. 37425 catches the autumn sunlight as it crosses Bassaleg Viaduct with its train, to load ballast at Machen Quarry. The viaduct, built in 1826, is believed to be the oldest operational example of its type in the world, having been constructed as part of the original 4ft 2in plate-way Rumney Railway. Built to connect Rhymney Ironworks to wharves at Newport Docks, this route, later converted to standard gauge, and run by the Brecon & Merthyr Jnc Railway (to be absorbed by GWR), was eventually truncated at Machen. 18 October 2002.

The Machen Quarry Branch is not known for many traditionally scenic views. In this case a tree provided the height to try and record a different landscape shot of a loaded Machen to ADJ ballast working, seen north of Rhiwderin, behind No. 37701. First allocated to Hull Dairycoates as D6730, a life in the north of England, and Scotland was followed by refurbishment from its No. 37030 guise to No. 37701, and allocation to Canton in 1986. The loco was scrapped in 2008. 29 October 1998.

Passing the village of Machen, this conveniently short train of only one Seacow hopper, behind No. 37197, fits into the small open section of line on the approach to the Quarry exchange sidings. New to Swansea Landore as D6897 in 1964, the loco was to leave Wales in favour of the north of England for 17 years before returning to Canton in 1984. Disposal came in 2012. 8 May 1996

The loading point at Machen Quarry, which at the time of writing is run by Hanson Aggregates, is the scene for former Class 03 D2199 hauling No. 37425's ADJ bound train towards the exchange sidings. The Quarry, established before 1875 to serve local lime kilns, is still an outlet for high quality crushed stone. 18 October 2002.

Another view of Bassaleg Viaduct, and the immaculate No. 37425, sees the loaded train featured in the previous view returning towards Park Junction. This particular working started from Newport East Usk Yard and loaded at Machen Quarry before returning to Alexandra Dock Junction (ADJ) Yard. New to Canton in 1965 as D6992, this locomotive features heavily in the book as it was very active around some of the Author's favourite Welsh 'haunts' during the early 'noughties'. Happily, it was still in service with Direct Rail Services at the time of writing. 18 October 2002.

The backdrop for this view of a westbound tank train is the now closed and redeveloped Pengam Freightliner Terminal. My records show that this shot was taken at just before 6 p.m., indicating that Nos 37162 and 37241 are hauling the 6V32 Albion to Waterston Gulf. 3 June 1992.

Seen approaching Splott Junction with 6Z57 – a train of reclaimed slag from Llanwern Steelworks – No. 37894 heads towards Cardiff Docks, where the train's contents were to be used as infill as part of the Cardiff Bay Development Project. Just visible to the left of the frame is part of Cardiff Tidal Sidings, beyond which Tremorfa Steelworks can be seen. 29 October 1998.

Dramatic December sunlight highlights Nos 37419 and 37425 top and tailing the 1Z37 Rhymney to Cardiff away from Ystrad Mynach. Sporting a headboard, this train was one of the final loco-hauled services along this route, ending the relatively short but welcome return of (mainly) Class 37s to the Valleys. 4 December 2005.

With loco-hauled trains due to cease in the Rhymney Valley six days hence, special motive power combinations were laid on to cover services to and from Cardiff. Here, Nos 50031 and 37411 top and tail 1Z32 from Cardiff, and are seen having just passed Ystrad Mynach Signal Box. In the following year Arriva Trains Wales (ATW) received complaints from commuters regarding comfort and overcrowding following the loss of loco-hauled trains. The result was the reinstatement of a morning and evening locomotive-hauled service, finally reverting to DMU in December 2006. 4 December 2005.

Rhymney line locomotive-hauled trains covered some peak-hour and Saturday services. In the spring of 2005, repaints were authorised on Nos 37425 and 37411, the former of which can be seen having just departed Ystrad Mynach with 2F34 Rhymney to Cardiff. The engine had yet to receive its *Pride of the Valleys* nameplates. 30 April 2005.

Freshly outshopped in large logo livery, No. 37425 approaches Ystrad Mynach with 2R42 Cardiff to Rhymney. The former No. 37292 looked very smart in a livery that it had carried in the mid-1980s, following refurbishment and conversion into a Class 37/4. 16 April 2005.

Near the end of the second decade of the twenty-first century, much of the coal traffic originating from South Wales centred on shipments from the Cwmbargoed Disposal Point (DP). Taken by Charlie Woollard, this view shows Freightliner's pioneer No. 66501 bring a Cwmbargoed to Grange Sidings loaded coal up to speed, having just gained the Rhymey line at Ystrad Mynach. Following its run down from the DP, this train had awaited onward passage between the busy schedule of ATW services to and from Bargoed and Rhymney to Cardiff. 5 April 2018.

Passing over the road to Nelson, No. 37425 is seen slowing for its stop at Ystrad Mynach station with a Saturday service from Rhymney to Cardiff. Out of sight, on the other side of the bridge, the line from Cwmbargoed joins the route to Cardiff, just south of the station. 12 April 2004.

This 2F34 Rhymney to Cardiff, hauled by No. 37425, is a hundred or so yards further along the line than the previous view at Ystrad Mynach as it nears the station platform. The huddle of photographers wishing to get this view of the still extant lower quadrant signals reminded the Author of images relating to the Royal Signals Motorcycle Display Team balancing act! 19 November 2005.

In 2000 the Rhymney loco-hauled services were still a relative novelty, producing slightly more in the way of haulage variety than the small pool of engines that later dominated services. In this case Transrail-liveried No. 37406 is seen Cardiff-bound, having just departed Bargoed station at 14.30. In the background is evidence of the then recently completed landscaping work involving the removal of the huge colliery tip associated with the nearby Bargoed Colliery. Originally sunk in 1912, and closed in 1977, this mine broke the world record for production of coal in a single shift in 1909 – just over 4,000 tons! 22 April 2000.

Heading away from Bargoed towards Gilfach, this Saturday Rhymney to Cardiff service is seen top and tailed by Nos 50031 and 50044. Motive power combinations like this encouraged enthusiasts from far and wide to come and enjoy a railway environment that had more in common with a heritage line than an important passenger route to the Welsh capital! 28 August 1999.

On a sunny November Saturday, No. 37425 – one of the regulars on these services – heads away from Bargoed with a Rhymney-bound train. The viaduct spans a valley that once saw the course of a line from Bargoed to Pant, and onwards, via Fochriw and Dowlais Top. 13 November 2004.

An immaculate No. 37408 is seen between Pontlottyn and Tir-Phil with a Cardiff-bound Saturday service. Sadly, this engine was withdrawn following collision damage sustained in a runaway situation at Rhymney Sidings. The other engine involved in the mishap, No. 37425, survived. Stored No. 37419 was reinstated to replace No. 37408. On the opposite side of the valley can be seen the village of Abertysswg. 6 April 2002.

The third line to radiate from Tondu is the one that heads west to Margam, which, until March 2009, saw trains to and from the huge opencast mine at Parc Slip, part way along its route. Following the closure of the mine, the sole purpose of this single line has been to continue as a diversionary route from the South Wales Main Line, as in this instance where the 6H32 10.24 Llanwern to Margam accelerates away from Tondu behind No. 60074. Later to receive a unique blue livery to highlight the work of the Teenage Cancer Trust, this loco was under DB ownership at the end of 2018. 29 January 2006.

Cantering past the junction to Margam Yard, No. 50049 makes light work of the four-coach 1B97 12.50 Fishguard to Cardiff on a Saturday in August 2006. The background is dominated by the Eglwys Nunydd Reservoir, originally constructed to provide cooling water for the cold rolling mills at Margam Steelworks. Also visible is the British Oxygen Company (BOC) industrial gases plant. From Margam, the South Wales Main Line runs roughly north-westwards to Briton Ferry before heading inland to Neath as part of its route to Swansea and beyond. 26 August 2006.

Part of the Margam and Port Talbot steel plants, together with No. 60064 waiting to join the main line with a coil train, form the backdrop for No. 56086 heading east with an unidentified train of covered steel wagons. A Doncaster product from 1980, this loco was scrapped at Kingsbury in 2013. 18 June 1999.

A recently ex-works No. 56044 is about to pass under the road access bridge to part of the rolling mill section of the Port Talbot Steelworks with the 6B26 Trostre to Margam. Named *Cardiff Canton Quality Assured* in 1992, it is sad to relate that this Doncaster product from 1978 was scrapped in 2007 at CF Booth, Rotherham. 27 August 1994.

The two giant operational blast furnaces of Port Talbot Steelworks, together with iron ore stocks (being augmented from the holds of a red bulk carrying ship), dominate the background as No. 56066 heads the 6B22 08.43 ADJ to Swansea Burrows Yard on a fine, clear day in July 1996. The train is conveying steel bar for export and two tank wagons for repair at Marcroft, near Burrows Yard. Then, as now, the massive complex consisted of these two ironmaking furnaces, together with the giant Abbey Basic Oxygen Steel (BOS) plant, a continuous casting (concast) plant and hot and cold rolling mills, together with the Grange coke ovens. 17 July 1996.

Passing the retaining wall for a long-disused rail flyover, No. 37803 heads away from Port Talbot with the 6E21 Baglan Bay to Humber propane tanks. Just to the right of the by then disused No. 3 Blast Furnace complex that dominates the background, the distant chimney of the Baglan Bay plant can just be seen. This engine was new to Landore in 1963 as D6908, later carrying the TOPS ID of No. 37208 before refurbishment to a Class 37/7. 7 July 1998.

An unidentified Class 60 appears dwarfed by the redundant Port Talbot No. 3 Blast Furnace as it heads the 6B26 Trostre to Margam coil empty towards its destination. There has been a long history of iron and steelmaking at Port Talbot and Margam Moors, with a number of plants in operation since 1901. Briefly, the original works, developed from 1901 to 1905, was joined by a Margam plant developed in the mid-1920s, followed by huge investment in the 1950s and '60s that saw the complex, which included the Abbey BOS plant, become the one-time biggest of its type in Europe. The No. 3 Blast Furnace, a product of the aforementioned post-war development, has since been demolished. 17 July 1996.

Just over half an hour after its booked departure time of 08.20, the 6E21 Baglan Bay to Humber propane tanks are seen approaching Port Talbot station behind No. 66115. In the background, above the then relatively new loco, can be seen the Baglan Bay Petrochemical Plant, from where the train originated. Opened by BP in 1963, within five years it had become one of the largest of its kind in Europe. However, market changes saw its rundown and closure between 1994 and 2004. 18 June 1999.

Briton Ferry is the location for this view of No. 56107 hauling the 7E10 Swansea Burrows to Immingham loaded coal. The train had just gained the main line at Court Sart Junction, just visible behind the last wagons. A regular Class 56 turn, this train always made an impressive sight (and sound!) when viewed across the Severn in the Author's native Gloucestershire – though, given the time of 18.37 for this shot, even in midsummer it would be dusk before the train appeared. A Doncaster product from 1982, No. 56107 was withdrawn in 2010 and scrapped the following year. 27 August 2002.

Though taken in uninspiringly dull conditions, this shot is included as, besides showing the full extent of Briton Ferry yard, much of the Baglan Bay Petrochemical Plant dominates the backdrop – before ten years of rundown saw it completely demolished. The subject is the 6C19 Aberthaw to Jersey Marine (Steel Supply) empty MGR, headed by Nos 37797 and 37897, which is to be loaded with blended coal for return to Aberthaw. In the yard can be seen a rake of MEAs loaded with recovered coal from Pontycymer, ready for the short trip to Steel Supply to add their contents to the blending stocks. 6 August 1994.

Another view looking north-west at Briton Ferry, this time showing a rake of bitumen tanks from Llandarcy Refinery accelerating away from Court Sart Junction behind No. 56004. At the time this picture was taken Llandarcy was in the process of closing, so it is unclear as to the identity of the train – the 6O70 to Grain in Kent being most likely. A busy Briton Ferry yard can be seen in the background, together with the station of the same name, just visible beyond the rakes of wagons. Built in Romania by Electroputere in 1977, No. 56004 was scrapped in 2006. Noteworthy was the fact the loco received new cabs due to collision damage, changing its appearance from that of the original batch of Electroputere engines. 7 July 1998.

The Saturday 6C32 Jersey Marine (Steel Supply) to Aberthaw MGR, hauled by Nos 37796 and 37895, is seen approaching Court Sart Junction and the South Wales Main Line. The train is passing under the former route of the South Wales Mineral Railway, dismantled as long ago as 1910, while itself taking a route opened by the Rhondda & Swansea Bay Railway (RSBR) in 1893. Of the two locos, No. 37895 can boast to have spent its first years in Wales, being new to Canton in 1963 as D6819. Transfer back to its first depot, following refurbishment from its guise as No. 37283, came in 1986. It was to be a stay of twelve years. 6 August 1994.

Built by the RSBR, the swing bridge over the River Neath near Skewen is the location for this view of No. 56003 heading the 6B22 08.43 ADJ to Burrows towards Dynevor Junction, Jersey Marine, and onwards to its destination. Records show that the bridge 'swung' fourteen times in 1947, reducing to once in 1956. Unsurprisingly, the bridge was welded shut as a cost-saving measure in later years. At the time of writing, the loco, built by Electroputere in 1977, was still in existence as No. 56312. 7 July 1998.

Unusually top and tailed, due to the failure of No. 37402, the late-running 1R38 Cardiff to Fishguard is seen crossing the River Neath Swing Bridge near Skewen under the power of No. 37419. The foreground is dominated by the rusting remains of *Light Vessel 72*. Built in 1903 for Trinity House, and withdrawn from service in the Bristol Channel in 1973, it was moved to this location – the quay for Steel Supply – for scrapping, until saved by the company's then manager. A contributory factor in its salvation may have been the ship's role in guiding British and Canadian troops through mine-swept channels to Juno Beach on D-Day in 1944. 16 August 2002.

With the route at Dynevor Junction set for the Swansea District Line, No. 60036 rumbles over the former RSBR Neath Swing Bridge with the Saturday 6B25 Westerleigh to Robeston empty fuel tanks. Completed as late as 1912, the District Line was built by the GWR with a view to ease congestion through Swansea following the then recent completion of the GWR route to Fishguard Harbour. The last main line built in Wales, the District Line offered easier gradients than the existing line via Neath and Skewen, linking with the RSBR route (by then run by the GWR) for its final section to Court Sart Junction at Briton Ferry. 30 March 1996.

The first three wagons of what is most likely the 7C12 Jersey Marine (Steel Supply) to Aberthaw are seen leaving their point of departure behind Nos 37894 and 37889. Beneath the threatening skies part of the town of Neath is visible, together with the two running lines combining before curving north-east to Dynevor Junction. The large buildings of Steel Supply dominate the right-hand side of the frame. As the name suggests the site had a history of involvement with metal recycling, though by the 1990s this had finished in favour of a concentration point for blending coal – chiefly for Aberthaw Power Station. 29 March 1996.

Seen in an earlier view leaving Briton Ferry yard, Nos 37797 and 37897 have split their train in the Steel Supply sidings, and loading is well under way on the first portion of what will become the 7C12 to Aberthaw. The bases of two 1930s vintage transmission pylons, used to span the River Neath, dominate the background. First allocated to Hull Dairycoates as D6781 in 1962, the lead loco spent much of its life in the north of England and Scotland until refurbishment from No. 37081 to No. 37797, and its eventual allocation to Canton by the time of this view. Disposal came in early 2006. 6 August 1994.

Thanks to kind permission being given to access the Steel Supply site, this alternative shot was possible, showing, as it does, the three loading shovels hard at work loading the first portion of 7C12 to Aberthaw. Just visible beyond the wagons are bridges for the two routes deviating from Dynevor Junction, the line from these sidings joining the nearest alignment, while the District Line continues westwards. Besides the aforementioned rail-delivered coal supplies, the site received much of its stock by road, both of which were suitably blended for Aberthaw's boilers. 6 August 1994.

Roughly midway between Dynevor Junction and Burrows Yard we see No. 37894 passing Jersey Marine with a Coedbach to Burrows coal, which went forward as the 6E15 to Doncaster Belmont. The Author's photographer companion on the day knew both the location for this shot and the fact that the train consist was a homogeneous rake of blue MEAs. As can be seen, his research paid off as the striking-looking train appeared in fine early evening light. Delivered new to Canton in 1963, and passing through the guise of D6824 and No. 37124, this engine, having moved to and from Wales in the ensuing twenty-three years, was allocated to Canton on its refurbishment in 1986, where it was based at the time of this photo. Disposal came in 2011. 8 May 1996.

Romanian Grid No. 56010 passes Jersey Marine with a Saturday 6C32 Cwmgwrach to Aberthaw MGR. The train is taking the former RSBR route to enable it to run round at Burrows Sidings. Completed in 1893/4 as part of a scheme to export Rhondda Fawr coal through the newly expanded Swansea Docks, the RSBR, much like the Barry Railway, aimed to avoid the congestion and delays associated with ports like Cardiff. New from Electroputere in July 1977, No. 56010 was scrapped in 2004. 10 September 1994.

Though having undergone considerable rationalisation in the years leading up to this view, Burrows Sidings, built to serve the nearby docks, could still be a busy place in the 1990s. Here, No. 47237 has just arrived at 15.00 with a trip of wagons that included tanks for repair at the nearby Port Tennant (Marcroft) wagon works. New from Brush in 1965, at the time of writing the loco survives under WCRC ownership. 7 October 1993.

Pictured en route from Burrows Sidings to the (now closed) Ford axle plant at Danygraig, No. 08994 is seen rubbing shoulders with road traffic during its short journey. Cut down in profile in order to work the former Burry Port and Gwendraeth lines, this Crewe product from 1958 carried the numbers D3577 and 08462 before assuming the identity shown. At the time of writing it was stored under HNRC ownership. 7 October 1993.

Continuing on from the previous view, No. 08994 is seen returning to Burrows Sidings with a trip of wagons from the Danygraig Ford plant. The sawtooth-roofed structure above the train was formerly Danygraig shed, closing to steam in 1960 and diesel in 1964. The structure was later leased to Gower Chemicals, the sidings of which can just be seen above the loco. At the time this company provided tank traffic that was staged from the adjacent sidings. 7 October 1993.

The cut-down nature of No. 08994's cab and body are apparent in this view of the loco preparing to set back into Burrows Sidings with the previously seen Ford components train. Though by 1993 the area had seen a sharp decline, there were still plenty of clues relating to its busy past. An example of this is the high voltage pylons to the right of the frame, inexorably linked with the former Tir John Power Station, which would have been out of sight to the left of the frame. When completed in 1936, this plant, designed to burn Welsh coal 'duff', was the largest of its type in the UK, being built for Swansea Corporation as part of a national initiative to combat unemployment by instigating National Grid infrastructure works. Latterly sporting three large chimneys, the plant closed in 1976. 7 October 1993.

Passing the remains of what was Swansea Dock Tin Yard, No. 09008 heads a trip of Port Talbot steel from Burrows Sidings for export from the nearby quay at Kings Dock, having just passed the junction of the same name. Behind the loco can be seen part of the now closed Aluminium Wire & Cable Company (AWCO) factory, part of which now houses Swansea Bus Museum. Built at Darlington in 1959, the former D3719 lasted in service to 2010. 10 January 1994.

By early 1994 Kings Dock Junction was very much a shadow of its former self, not least due to a decline steepened by the cessation of coal exports through the nearby Kings Dock in 1987. Here No. 09008 picks its way through largely redundant trackwork as it returns to Burrows Yard with empty steel wagons, the contents of which had been shipped at the nearby quay. Completed in 1909, the 72-acre Kings Dock was built to meet the growing demand for tinplate exports from the surrounding area, as well as handling coal exports via hoists that, as little as seven to ten years before this shot was taken, would have dominated the backdrop. 10 January 1994.

This view shows No. 09008 approaching Swansea Kings Dock to pick up empty bolster wagons, visible beneath the cranes, for Burrows Yard. To the south of this dock, the construction of a large breakwater in the Bristol Channel eventually formed an enclosed section of water that became Queens Dock. Opened in 1920, this dock handled petroleum products from the newly opened Llandarcy Refinery – the first of its kind in the UK. 10 January 1994.

Seemingly emerging from the trees, No. 56119 slowly accelerates the 6C32 12.12 Cwmgwrach to Aberthaw towards Neath and Brecon Junction. Having worked down the surviving western section of the former Vale of Neath Railway, from the Unity Drift Mine at Cwmgwrach, the train will pass through Jersey Marine South Junction before arriving at Burrows Sidings to run round, prior to continuing its journey to the power station. The then little-used line to Onllwyn can be seen to the left of the train. The loco, new from Crewe Works in 1983, was one of a handful of the class then based in South Wales. Withdrawal and scrapping came in 2010/11. 20 August 1994.

Spring sunshine highlights Nos 37896 and 37898 heading the SO 6C06 08.30 Aberthaw to Cwmgwrach between Neath and Aberdulais. Just visible in the distance, beyond the work taking place for the A465 upgrade, is some of the remaining part of the Llandarcy Oil Refinery. This complex, originally opened in 1922, was Britain's first large-scale refinery site, developed by the Anglo Persian Oil Company – later to become British Petroleum (BP). Total closure of the premises came in 1998. 30 March 1996.

Headed by No. 56076, the 12.12 6C32 Cwmgwrach to Aberthaw is seen passing the site of Aberdulais Halt, the remaining platform of which, hidden by the train's consist, was still extant at the time of the view. Closed in June 1964, this halt was one of several stations on the former Vale of Neath Railway route which originally linked Merthyr with the docks at Swansea. The broad top to the embankment may be a clue to the fact that this line was originally laid in broad gauge. Work on upgrading the A465 trunk road can be seen taking place in the background. 8 May 1996.

The loaded 6C32 to Aberthaw is seen again, this time passing the village of Clyne, behind South Wales regulars Nos 37896 and 37898. The latter loco, new to Swansea Landore as D6886 in November 1963, was to spend much of its life in South Wales, carrying the TOPS ID of No. 37186 prior to refurbishment to the 37/7 variant seen in this view. Withdrawal and scrapping came in 2010 and 2011 respectively. Again, evidence of the new alignment of the A465 Neath to Abergavenny Trunk Road is a feature of the backdrop, behind the trees. 30 March 1996.

The empty (6C06) working that was to form the train in the previous shot is seen passing the village of Resolven on its way up to the Cwmgwrach Drift Mine. Despite having to use the 'old' A465 route, the Author managed to successfully chase this empty train from the previous view of it further down the line near Aberdulais. It has to be said, however, that operating issues for the traincrew, associated with a manual level crossing at Clyne, had more than a small part to play in the success of this move! 30 March 1996.

The 'Christopher's Express' charter of September 1999 started and finished in Barry taking in, among other places, the Cynon and Rhondda valleys. It is in the latter valley that Nos 37407 and 37417 are seen at either end of the train, departing Porth station as they head for Pontypridd, prior to reversing for the northbound journey to Abercynon and beyond. Porth, where the two tributaries of the River Rhondda meet, sees itself as the unofficial capital of the Rhondda. 12 September 1999.

By the turn of the twentieth/twenty-first centuries, only the former Taff Valley Railway route up the Rhondda Fawr to Treherbert remained in use, the line up the Rhondda Fach having fallen into disuse with the demise of the last Rhondda mine, Maerdy, ten or so years before. Unsurprisingly, the history of the Rhondda Valleys is inexorably linked with the coal industry, with the peak years of output being between 1840 and 1925. The total number of mines peaked at seventy-five in 1893, with a massive 9.6 million tons of coal exported from the area in 1913. No. 37407 leads the 'Christopher's Express' charter and No. 37417 down the Rhondda Fawr, between Tonypandy and Porth, on a fine Sunday in September 1999. The River Rhondda can be seen to the left of the frame. 12 September 1999.

At 14.35, with the descent of both the Taff Bargoed and Rhymney valleys behind it, together with negotiating the Cardiff area, the 7C07 Cwmbargoed to Aberthaw storms through Eastbrook behind Nos 37896 and 37889. The rail route from Cardiff that this hard-working pair of Class 37s is using owes its origins to the Taff Vale Railway (to Cogan Junction), and the Barry Railway henceforth. 19 March 1995.

The 6M45 Barry to Burn Naze slowly negotiates the tracks to the east of the Barry Docks complex behind Transrail Dutch-liveried No. 56036. At the time of writing, this locomotive – the first to wear the large logo scheme in June 1979 – was awaiting disposal. The train was loaded at the Dow Corning Chemical Plant, part of which can be seen in the background. This works, an important producer of silicones, was undergoing huge investment at the time of the photograph. The vantage point was an old lighting tower, shown to the Author by a local photographer. 12 April 1997.

With the lighting tower vantage point for the previous view just visible beyond Barry No. 2 Dock's then still extant cranes, No. 56119 is seen heading the 6M45 to Burn Naze empty vinyl chloride monomer (VCM) tanks away from its point of origin, visible on the horizon. The locomotive entered into traffic in May 1983, withdrawal coming in July 2010. 26 June 1995.

No. 37886 catches the sun as it follows the course of Barry No. 2 Dock with the 6B07 trip to Alexandra Dock Junction (ADJ). Barry Docks were opened between 1889 and 1898 as an alternative to the congested and expensive Cardiff Docks – chiefly for the export of coal from the Welsh Valleys. Coal shipped through Barry peaked in 1913, with just over 11 million tons exported from a South Wales total of 56 million tons. Besides coal, the Geest company used the port from 1959 to the 1980s to import West Indian bananas. The Author well remembers seeing the large, imposing white Geest ships there during visits with his father in the late 1970s. 3 August 2001.

The ADJ trip working is seen again, about to cross one of the dock roads as it heads inland towards the junction with the main line. Note the iconic styling of both the Class 37 and the Mercedes car. It could be argued that the venerable EE Type 3's appearance was already outdated by the time of its development sharing, as it did, many body parts from the then EE Type 4 (Class 40) production run. Styling issues aside, history shows how successful this rugged and dependable type has been, with a large number allocated to South Wales depots in the '60s and '70s, before gradually drifting away in subsequent years. 3 August 2001.

Passing over the causeway section from Barry Town to Barry Island station, the 'Christopher's Express' charter, seen previously in the Rhondda Valley, heads towards its point of departure, top and tailed by Nos 37407 and 37417. Out of sight of this view to the right, the 'West Pond' area was once the location for Woodham Brothers' sidings, famous for at one time holding up to 297 withdrawn steam locos. Happily, 213 survived into preservation which, alas, was a fate that did not befall the two North British-built diesel residents, D601 *Ark Royal* and D6122, which were scrapped in 1980. The Author remembers climbing through their faded green, stripped hulks in 1979 noting, among other things, the quality of the workmanship on the aluminium bodywork – especially around the cabs. Their demise was very sad, having nearly made it into an era where extinct locomotive types are virtually scratch built... 12 September 1999.

After recording the previous image of 7C07 passing Eastbrook, Nos 37896 and 37889 can be seen blasting through Barry Town station under clear signals en route to Aberthaw. Much of the town, which once bordered up to 100 miles of siding space for the dock complex, can be seen in the background. Also just visible to the right is the entrance to the former Motive Power Depot which, at the time of the photo, was the main wagon repair facility for the South Wales area. 19 March 1995.

Midwinter sunshine at Barry highlights No. 37675 heading the 6B89 Cardiff Tidal to Aberthaw Power Station fuel tanks. One of the main uses of fuel oil at a coal power station is boiler start up, where the pulverised coal blown into the boiler has to be ignited by an oil-fired pilot flame. The lines to Barry Island can be seen deviating to the right, with the train heading on to the Vale of Glamorgan (VOG) route, from Barry to Bridgend. Opened in 1897, the VOG line, underwritten by the Barry Railway, provided access to Barry Docks for Llynfi, Garw and Ogmore Valley coal output. 28 December 2001.

The imposing structure of Porthkerry Viaduct, between Barry and Aberthaw, is the most significant piece of civil engineering on the VOG line. In early evening September sunlight that makes the Bristol Channel look almost Mediterranean, the diverted 6B33 Theale to Robeston empty tanks heads west behind No. 60019. Interestingly, on opening for traffic the viaduct suffered serious subsidence problems, requiring a temporary bypass line for three years to keep the route open until partial reconstruction was completed in 1900. 9 September 2006.

Passing the fine signal gantry protecting the westbound approach to Aberthaw, Nos 43191 and 43015 power a diverted Swansea to Paddington HST towards Rhoose and Barry. Then still some eight years away from the return of a scheduled passenger service, the VOG line saw frequent use by all trains as a diversionary route from the South Wales Main Line often, as here, due to Sunday engineering work. 13 April 1997.

The substantial heat haze from the roof of No. 56076 is ample evidence of the effort required to move the well-loaded diverted 6M84 Margam to Dee Marsh up the 1 in 200 away from Aberthaw on a cold Sunday in March 1995. Note the disused platforms of the old station, and the relief of the signalman returning to the warmth of his signal box after watching the train pass! 19 March 1995.

The Cardiff Tidal to Aberthaw Power Station tanks, seen previously at Barry, takes the double track loop to the power station circuit behind No. 37675. Built on the site of a golf course, Aberthaw 'A' plant officially opened in 1963, generating until 1995. In 1971 the adjacent 1,500 megawatt 'B' site was opened, considerably increasing the importance of the VOG line from the point of view of coal, and to a lesser extent oil movements to the site. Designed to burn pulverised coal, and fitted with desulphurising plant from 2006, at the time of writing Aberthaw 'B' co-fires biomass and imported coal. 28 December 2001.

Diverted via the VOG due to engineering work, the Saturday 1B97 Fishguard to Cardiff is seen passing Aberthaw behind No. 50049 *Defiance*. Looking from the opposite direction to the previous shot, this view clearly shows the sharply curved nature of the route at this location. 9 September 2006.

Having run round their train of blended coal from Steel Supply, Jersey Marine, Nos 37896 and 87802 head towards the Aberthaw Power Station loop to begin the discharge – or 'tip' as the local traincrews called it – of their load to the site bunkers or coal stocks. Seen in the background is part of the considerable quarry workings at Aberthaw, an important source of 'hydraulic' limestone used, among other things, in the production of cement. 8 October 1994.

The train seen in the previous view, hauled by Coal Sector-liveried Nos 37896 and 37802, is dwarfed by the massive Aberthaw Cement Works as it heads towards the power station discharge loop. By this time the only remaining such plant on the VOG, the Rhoose works having closed in 1987, the Aberthaw complex evolved from kilns opened in 1914, which were augmented and/or replaced from just after the Second World War until 1975. The aforementioned supply of limestone together with access to Welsh coal made the site an ideal location for cement production. The works continues in operation at the time of writing. 8 October 1994.

Heading west from Aberthaw behind No. 37902, the 6B15 Barry to Baglan Bay chemical tanks approaches St Athan. In the background, besides the Aberthaw Cement Works, part of the Cardiff Airport complex dominates the horizon. Delivered new to Cardiff Canton in 1963 as D6848, a transfer to Scotland in 1968 was followed by renumbering to 37148 in 1974. Further moves between these two countries was followed by overhaul and conversion to a Class 37/9 in 1986, which involved fitting a new Mirrlees engine, Brush alternator, refurbished bogies and ballasting to 120 tons. The loco returned to Canton, where it was allocated at the time of this view. 23 June 1995.

This last view from the VOG line is of a diverted Sunday 6M30 Margam to Dee Marsh coil, headed by a No. 60033 yet to gain its celebrity status via British Steel blue and Corus silver repaints. Under dramatic skies, the train is seen passing part of the RAF (later MOD) St Athan site. Opened in 1938, the base is still operational in late 2018 – chiefly as a technical training facility. 26 February 1995.

The South Wales Main Line at Miskin, between Pontyclun and Peterston-super-Ely, is the location for this view of No. 56032 hauling the 6B54 Grange Sidings to Llanwern loaded coal. Built at Doncaster in 1977, this engine was named *Sir De Morgannwg/County of South Glamorgan* in 1983. At the time of writing No. 56032 is stored, under the ownership of GBRf. 8 February 1996.

Heading south between Sarn and Litchard on the Tondu to Bridgend line is a diverted 6M41 Margam to Round Oak steel, hauled by No. 66091. The train is taking a route that opened in 1864 by the Llnyvi Valley Railway (LVR). At the time of writing in late 2018, the former steelworks site at Round Oak, near Birmingham, was still a regular recipient of Welsh steel products. 29 January 2006.

Waiting for the right of way at Tondu at 08.30 on a bitterly cold day in early December 1992, No. 37899 sits at the head of a rake of MEAs to be loaded with reclaimed coal at the former Maesteg Washery site. It is sad to relate that this loco, delivered new to Swansea Landore as D6861 in 1963, was scrapped in Madrid, Spain, in July 2003. This engine was the highest numbered Class 37/7, being refurbished to No. 37899 from its TOPS ID of No. 37161. 8 December 1992.

By the time of this view the remaining part of the Garw Valley Line, built under the supervision of the GWR in 1876, and the former LVR route to Maesteg were the only routes left radiating northwards from Tondu. It is on the former route that we see No. 37903 heading towards Pantygog with the 7B63 empty MEAs to load reclaimed coal at Pontycymer. On this still March morning, the horn tones for the numerous foot crossings, together with the sound of No. 37903's (by then) poorly silenced Mirlees engine, could be heard long before the train appeared, such was the audio effect of the steep-sided valley. 22 March 1995.

Following on from the previous image, No. 37903 has run round its train and set back into the last remaining stub of the Garw Valley Line, situated at Pontycymer. A land reclamation scheme, from which previously discarded coal was recovered, removed the last mile of the route to Blaengarw where, up to 1985, a colliery was in operation. Large dumper trucks conveyed reclaimed coal to this pad, where loading of the 7B65 to Steel Supply, Jersey Marine, has just commenced. At its destination the coal was blended with stocks from other sources, such as Cwmgwrach in the Vale of Neath, before conveyance to Aberthaw Power Station. 22 March 1995.

To continue the sequence of shots taken in March 1995, the loaded 7B65 is seen heading past Pantygog at the beginning of its journey to Jersey Marine. In the guise of D6949, Nos 37249 and 37903, the train engine was allocated to Cardiff Canton, Healey Mills, Gateshead, Thornaby, Tinsley and back to Canton where it was allocated at the time this photograph was taken. The late running of this train meant the light angle was perfect to record a well-known view that, to many, epitomises a South Wales valley railway scene. 22 March 1995.

A final view of 7B65, and the Garw Valley, sees the train passing Pontyrhyl as it heads towards Tondu. After the last coal train ran in 1986, the line fell into disuse until reopening in the early 1990s to serve the aforementioned reclamation scheme. The 'Garw Guru' charter of April 1997, following the previous month's last train of coal, was the final train to use the line which, though severed and missing bridge infrastructure, was the subject of a preservation project at the time of writing. 22 March 1995.

This train, seen in a previous shot at Tondu, was one of the last run to recover coal from the former Maesteg Washery site. No. 37899 raises the roofs of Maesteg as it lifts the empty MEA consist up to the loop and washery connection. By the time this picture was taken, Maesteg was the end point of the former Llyfi Valley Railway route that had seen its first mineral trains in 1861, followed by passenger services in 1864. Finishing in 1970, passenger trains had returned to Maesteg in September 1992, three months before this scene was recorded. 8 December 1992.

With the line from Maesteg visible to the right of the frame, No. 37899 carefully propels its train up the gradient towards the former washery loading pad. The Author was fortunate to have friends that put a lot of effort into researching the running of trains like this, enabling trips to be arranged to record scenes that were by then rapidly disappearing. Certainly where the Welsh Valleys were concerned, a feeling of 'picking over the remains' of once vibrant industrial railways permeated the period covered by this book. 8 December 1992.

In a view that epitomises the desolation to be found at the site of the former Maesteg Washery, an excavator has just begun to load No. 37899's MEA consist with recovered coal destined for blending at Steel Supply, Jersey Marine. The washery was opened in 1957 to process coal from local collieries. Following closure in 1989, the site was gradually cleared of infrastructure, with little visible at the end of 1992. 8 December 1992.

The town of Maesteg forms the backdrop for the loaded train descending from the remains of the washery site. On re-joining the remaining stub of the Maesteg line, the train would run round and pass below the former Pont-y-Rhyl to Port Talbot Central, Aberavon Town and onwards route, visible above the train. Midwinter sunlight, and the output from numerous coal-burning fires as a result of the cold conditions, added to an atmosphere that, arguably, provided a visual link with the area's past. 8 December 1992.

The third line to radiate from Tondu is the one that heads west to Margam, which, until March 2009, saw trains to and from the huge opencast mine at Parc Slip, part way along its route. Following the closure of the mine, the sole purpose of this single line has been to continue as a diversionary route from the South Wales Main Line, as in this instance where the 6H32 10.24 Llanwern to Margam accelerates away from Tondu behind No. 60074. Later to receive a unique blue livery to highlight the work of the Teenage Cancer Trust, this loco was under DB ownership at the end of 2018. 29 January 2006.

Cantering past the junction to Margam Yard, No. 50049 makes light work of the four-coach 1B97 12.50 Fishguard to Cardiff on a Saturday in August 2006. The background is dominated by the Eglwys Nunydd Reservoir, originally constructed to provide cooling water for the cold rolling mills at Margam Steelworks. Also visible is the British Oxygen Company (BOC) industrial gases plant. From Margam, the South Wales Main Line runs roughly north-westwards to Briton Ferry before heading inland to Neath as part of its route to Swansea and beyond. 26 August 2006.

Part of the Margam and Port Talbot steel plants, together with No. 60064 waiting to join the main line with a coil train, form the backdrop for No. 56086 heading east with an unidentified train of covered steel wagons. A Doncaster product from 1980, this loco was scrapped at Kingsbury in 2013. 18 June 1999.

A recently ex-works No. 56044 is about to pass under the road access bridge to part of the rolling mill section of the Port Talbot Steelworks with the 6B26 Trostre to Margam. Named *Cardiff Canton Quality Assured* in 1992, it is sad to relate that this Doncaster product from 1978 was scrapped in 2007 at CF Booth, Rotherham. 27 August 1994.

The two giant operational blast furnaces of Port Talbot Steelworks, together with iron ore stocks (being augmented from the holds of a red bulk carrying ship), dominate the background as No. 56066 heads the 6B22 08.43 ADJ to Swansea Burrows Yard on a fine, clear day in July 1996. The train is conveying steel bar for export and two tank wagons for repair at Marcroft, near Burrows Yard. Then, as now, the massive complex consisted of these two ironmaking furnaces, together with the giant Abbey Basic Oxygen Steel (BOS) plant, a continuous casting (concast) plant and hot and cold rolling mills, together with the Grange coke ovens. 17 July 1996.

Passing the retaining wall for a long-disused rail flyover, No. 37803 heads away from Port Talbot with the 6E21 Baglan Bay to Humber propane tanks. Just to the right of the by then disused No. 3 Blast Furnace complex that dominates the background, the distant chimney of the Baglan Bay plant can just be seen. This engine was new to Landore in 1963 as D6908, later carrying the TOPS ID of No. 37208 before refurbishment to a Class 37/7. 7 July 1998.

An unidentified Class 60 appears dwarfed by the redundant Port Talbot No. 3 Blast Furnace as it heads the 6B26 Trostre to Margam coil empty towards its destination. There has been a long history of iron and steelmaking at Port Talbot and Margam Moors, with a number of plants in operation since 1901. Briefly, the original works, developed from 1901 to 1905, was joined by a Margam plant developed in the mid-1920s, followed by huge investment in the 1950s and '60s that saw the complex, which included the Abbey BOS plant, become the one-time biggest of its type in Europe. The No. 3 Blast Furnace, a product of the aforementioned post-war development, has since been demolished. 17 July 1996.

Just over half an hour after its booked departure time of 08.20, the 6E21 Baglan Bay to Humber propane tanks are seen approaching Port Talbot station behind No. 66115. In the background, above the then relatively new loco, can be seen the Baglan Bay Petrochemical Plant, from where the train originated. Opened by BP in 1963, within five years it had become one of the largest of its kind in Europe. However, market changes saw its rundown and closure between 1994 and 2004. 18 June 1999.

Briton Ferry is the location for this view of No. 56107 hauling the 7E10 Swansea Burrows to Immingham loaded coal. The train had just gained the main line at Court Sart Junction, just visible behind the last wagons. A regular Class 56 turn, this train always made an impressive sight (and sound!) when viewed across the Severn in the Author's native Gloucestershire – though, given the time of 18.37 for this shot, even in midsummer it would be dusk before the train appeared. A Doncaster product from 1982, No. 56107 was withdrawn in 2010 and scrapped the following year. 27 August 2002.

Though taken in uninspiringly dull conditions, this shot is included as, besides showing the full extent of Briton Ferry yard, much of the Baglan Bay Petrochemical Plant dominates the backdrop – before ten years of rundown saw it completely demolished. The subject is the 6C19 Aberthaw to Jersey Marine (Steel Supply) empty MGR, headed by Nos 37797 and 37897, which is to be loaded with blended coal for return to Aberthaw. In the yard can be seen a rake of MEAs loaded with recovered coal from Pontycymer, ready for the short trip to Steel Supply to add their contents to the blending stocks. 6 August 1994.

Another view looking north-west at Briton Ferry, this time showing a rake of bitumen tanks from Llandarcy Refinery accelerating away from Court Sart Junction behind No. 56004. At the time this picture was taken Llandarcy was in the process of closing, so it is unclear as to the identity of the train – the 6O70 to Grain in Kent being most likely. A busy Briton Ferry yard can be seen in the background, together with the station of the same name, just visible beyond the rakes of wagons. Built in Romania by Electroputere in 1977, No. 56004 was scrapped in 2006. Noteworthy was the fact the loco received new cabs due to collision damage, changing its appearance from that of the original batch of Electroputere engines. 7 July 1998.

The Saturday 6C32 Jersey Marine (Steel Supply) to Aberthaw MGR, hauled by Nos 37796 and 37895, is seen approaching Court Sart Junction and the South Wales Main Line. The train is passing under the former route of the South Wales Mineral Railway, dismantled as long ago as 1910, while itself taking a route opened by the Rhondda & Swansea Bay Railway (RSBR) in 1893. Of the two locos, No. 37895 can boast to have spent its first years in Wales, being new to Canton in 1963 as D6819. Transfer back to its first depot, following refurbishment from its guise as No. 37283, came in 1986. It was to be a stay of twelve years. 6 August 1994.

Built by the RSBR, the swing bridge over the River Neath near Skewen is the location for this view of No. 56003 heading the 6B22 08.43 ADJ to Burrows towards Dynevor Junction, Jersey Marine, and onwards to its destination. Records show that the bridge 'swung' fourteen times in 1947, reducing to once in 1956. Unsurprisingly, the bridge was welded shut as a cost-saving measure in later years. At the time of writing, the loco, built by Electroputere in 1977, was still in existence as No. 56312. 7 July 1998.

Unusually top and tailed, due to the failure of No. 37402, the late-running 1R38 Cardiff to Fishguard is seen crossing the River Neath Swing Bridge near Skewen under the power of No. 37419. The foreground is dominated by the rusting remains of *Light Vessel 72*. Built in 1903 for Trinity House, and withdrawn from service in the Bristol Channel in 1973, it was moved to this location – the quay for Steel Supply – for scrapping, until saved by the company's then manager. A contributory factor in its salvation may have been the ship's role in guiding British and Canadian troops through mine-swept channels to Juno Beach on D-Day in 1944. 16 August 2002.

With the route at Dynevor Junction set for the Swansea District Line, No. 60036 rumbles over the former RSBR Neath Swing Bridge with the Saturday 6B25 Westerleigh to Robeston empty fuel tanks. Completed as late as 1912, the District Line was built by the GWR with a view to ease congestion through Swansea following the then recent completion of the GWR route to Fishguard Harbour. The last main line built in Wales, the District Line offered easier gradients than the existing line via Neath and Skewen, linking with the RSBR route (by then run by the GWR) for its final section to Court Sart Junction at Briton Ferry. 30 March 1996.

The first three wagons of what is most likely the 7C12 Jersey Marine (Steel Supply) to Aberthaw are seen leaving their point of departure behind Nos 37894 and 37889. Beneath the threatening skies part of the town of Neath is visible, together with the two running lines combining before curving north-east to Dynevor Junction. The large buildings of Steel Supply dominate the right-hand side of the frame. As the name suggests the site had a history of involvement with metal recycling, though by the 1990s this had finished in favour of a concentration point for blending coal – chiefly for Aberthaw Power Station. 29 March 1996.

Seen in an earlier view leaving Briton Ferry yard, Nos 37797 and 37897 have split their train in the Steel Supply sidings, and loading is well under way on the first portion of what will become the 7C12 to Aberthaw. The bases of two 1930s vintage transmission pylons, used to span the River Neath, dominate the background. First allocated to Hull Dairycoates as D6781 in 1962, the lead loco spent much of its life in the north of England and Scotland until refurbishment from No. 37081 to No. 37797, and its eventual allocation to Canton by the time of this view. Disposal came in early 2006. 6 August 1994.

Thanks to kind permission being given to access the Steel Supply site, this alternative shot was possible, showing, as it does, the three loading shovels hard at work loading the first portion of 7C12 to Aberthaw. Just visible beyond the wagons are bridges for the two routes deviating from Dynevor Junction, the line from these sidings joining the nearest alignment, while the District Line continues westwards. Besides the aforementioned rail-delivered coal supplies, the site received much of its stock by road, both of which were suitably blended for Aberthaw's boilers. 6 August 1994.

Roughly midway between Dynevor Junction and Burrows Yard we see No. 37894 passing Jersey Marine with a Coedbach to Burrows coal, which went forward as the 6E15 to Doncaster Belmont. The Author's photographer companion on the day knew both the location for this shot and the fact that the train consist was a homogeneous rake of blue MEAs. As can be seen, his research paid off as the striking-looking train appeared in fine early evening light. Delivered new to Canton in 1963, and passing through the guise of D6824 and No. 37124, this engine, having moved to and from Wales in the ensuing twenty-three years, was allocated to Canton on its refurbishment in 1986, where it was based at the time of this photo. Disposal came in 2011. 8 May 1996.

Romanian Grid No. 56010 passes Jersey Marine with a Saturday 6C32 Cwmgwrach to Aberthaw MGR. The train is taking the former RSBR route to enable it to run round at Burrows Sidings. Completed in 1893/4 as part of a scheme to export Rhondda Fawr coal through the newly expanded Swansea Docks, the RSBR, much like the Barry Railway, aimed to avoid the congestion and delays associated with ports like Cardiff. New from Electroputere in July 1977, No. 56010 was scrapped in 2004. 10 September 1994.

Though having undergone considerable rationalisation in the years leading up to this view, Burrows Sidings, built to serve the nearby docks, could still be a busy place in the 1990s. Here, No. 47237 has just arrived at 15.00 with a trip of wagons that included tanks for repair at the nearby Port Tennant (Marcroft) wagon works. New from Brush in 1965, at the time of writing the loco survives under WCRC ownership. 7 October 1993.

Pictured en route from Burrows Sidings to the (now closed) Ford axle plant at Danygraig, No. 08994 is seen rubbing shoulders with road traffic during its short journey. Cut down in profile in order to work the former Burry Port and Gwendraeth lines, this Crewe product from 1958 carried the numbers D3577 and 08462 before assuming the identity shown. At the time of writing it was stored under HNRC ownership. 7 October 1993.

Continuing on from the previous view, No. 08994 is seen returning to Burrows Sidings with a trip of wagons from the Danygraig Ford plant. The sawtooth-roofed structure above the train was formerly Danygraig shed, closing to steam in 1960 and diesel in 1964. The structure was later leased to Gower Chemicals, the sidings of which can just be seen above the loco. At the time this company provided tank traffic that was staged from the adjacent sidings. 7 October 1993.

The cut-down nature of No. 08994's cab and body are apparent in this view of the loco preparing to set back into Burrows Sidings with the previously seen Ford components train. Though by 1993 the area had seen a sharp decline, there were still plenty of clues relating to its busy past. An example of this is the high voltage pylons to the right of the frame, inexorably linked with the former Tir John Power Station, which would have been out of sight to the left of the frame. When completed in 1936, this plant, designed to burn Welsh coal 'duff', was the largest of its type in the UK, being built for Swansea Corporation as part of a national initiative to combat unemployment by instigating National Grid infrastructure works. Latterly sporting three large chimneys, the plant closed in 1976. 7 October 1993.

Passing the remains of what was Swansea Dock Tin Yard, No. 09008 heads a trip of Port Talbot steel from Burrows Sidings for export from the nearby quay at Kings Dock, having just passed the junction of the same name. Behind the loco can be seen part of the now closed Aluminium Wire & Cable Company (AWCO) factory, part of which now houses Swansea Bus Museum. Built at Darlington in 1959, the former D3719 lasted in service to 2010. 10 January 1994.

By early 1994 Kings Dock Junction was very much a shadow of its former self, not least due to a decline steepened by the cessation of coal exports through the nearby Kings Dock in 1987. Here No. 09008 picks its way through largely redundant trackwork as it returns to Burrows Yard with empty steel wagons, the contents of which had been shipped at the nearby quay. Completed in 1909, the 72-acre Kings Dock was built to meet the growing demand for tinplate exports from the surrounding area, as well as handling coal exports via hoists that, as little as seven to ten years before this shot was taken, would have dominated the backdrop. 10 January 1994.

This view shows No. 09008 approaching Swansea Kings Dock to pick up empty bolster wagons, visible beneath the cranes, for Burrows Yard. To the south of this dock, the construction of a large breakwater in the Bristol Channel eventually formed an enclosed section of water that became Queens Dock. Opened in 1920, this dock handled petroleum products from the newly opened Llandarcy Refinery – the first of its kind in the UK. 10 January 1994.

Seemingly emerging from the trees, No. 56119 slowly accelerates the 6C32 12.12 Cwmgwrach to Aberthaw towards Neath and Brecon Junction. Having worked down the surviving western section of the former Vale of Neath Railway, from the Unity Drift Mine at Cwmgwrach, the train will pass through Jersey Marine South Junction before arriving at Burrows Sidings to run round, prior to continuing its journey to the power station. The then little-used line to Onllwyn can be seen to the left of the train. The loco, new from Crewe Works in 1983, was one of a handful of the class then based in South Wales. Withdrawal and scrapping came in 2010/11. 20 August 1994.

Spring sunshine highlights Nos 37896 and 37898 heading the SO 6C06 08.30 Aberthaw to Cwmgwrach between Neath and Aberdulais. Just visible in the distance, beyond the work taking place for the A465 upgrade, is some of the remaining part of the Llandarcy Oil Refinery. This complex, originally opened in 1922, was Britain's first large-scale refinery site, developed by the Anglo Persian Oil Company – later to become British Petroleum (BP). Total closure of the premises came in 1998. 30 March 1996.

Headed by No. 56076, the 12.12 6C32 Cwmgwrach to Aberthaw is seen passing the site of Aberdulais Halt, the remaining platform of which, hidden by the train's consist, was still extant at the time of the view. Closed in June 1964, this halt was one of several stations on the former Vale of Neath Railway route which originally linked Merthyr with the docks at Swansea. The broad top to the embankment may be a clue to the fact that this line was originally laid in broad gauge. Work on upgrading the A465 trunk road can be seen taking place in the background. 8 May 1996.

The loaded 6C32 to Aberthaw is seen again, this time passing the village of Clyne, behind South Wales regulars Nos 37896 and 37898. The latter loco, new to Swansea Landore as D6886 in November 1963, was to spend much of its life in South Wales, carrying the TOPS ID of No. 37186 prior to refurbishment to the 37/7 variant seen in this view. Withdrawal and scrapping came in 2010 and 2011 respectively. Again, evidence of the new alignment of the A465 Neath to Abergavenny Trunk Road is a feature of the backdrop, behind the trees. 30 March 1996.

The empty (6C06) working that was to form the train in the previous shot is seen passing the village of Resolven on its way up to the Cwmgwrach Drift Mine. Despite having to use the 'old' A465 route, the Author managed to successfully chase this empty train from the previous view of it further down the line near Aberdulais. It has to be said, however, that operating issues for the traincrew, associated with a manual level crossing at Clyne, had more than a small part to play in the success of this move! 30 March 1996.

Romanian-built No. 56007 passes through Resolven with the Saturday 6C32 to Aberthaw in fine May sunshine that, among other things, highlights the flags and bunting in the adjacent street that had been used to commemorate the 50th anniversary of VE Day, five days earlier. The fluctuating fortunes of this surviving part of the Vale of Neath Railway route were, and are, inexorably linked to those of the local mining industry. As an example, some months before the date of this view a friend had recorded substantial tree growth between the sleepers at this particular location! The reopening of the drift mine at Cwmgwrach (often referred to as Aberpergwm) in the mid-1990s saw the track cleared and repaired in preparation for new traffic. New in April 1977, No. 56007 had been acquired by GBRf at the time of writing. 13 May 1995.

The 6C32 12.12 Cwmgwrach to Aberthaw makes a thunderous approach to Resolven behind Nos 37802 and 37898. Barely 3 miles into its journey from the then resurgent drift mine, 6C32 can once again be seen near to the new A465 alignment that was to open later that year. No stranger to the pages of this book, the leading loco was to start its working life from Landore as D6863 in August 1963. An eighteen-year absence from Wales ended in 1984 with the engine returning to Canton as No. 37163. Two years later 37/7 refurbishment saw the loco working off the Cardiff depot in the guise seen here. Disposal came in Spain in July 2003. 12 June 1996.

Mechanical shovels can be seen making short work of loading the 12.12 departure from Cwmgwrach to Aberthaw, hauled by No. 56007. Then known as the Unity Drift Mine, this colliery restarted production in the 1990s on a site that had been closed by the NCB in 1985. More commonly known as Aberpergwm, drift mines had been worked here since the nineteenth century, supplying good quality anthracite – latterly for power generation. Subsequent to the 1990s, shipments to Aberthaw gave way to supplying Tata Steel's Port Talbot works – a flow which ceased in 2015. At the time of writing, discussions were under way to return the site to production from its 'care and maintenance' status. 13 May 1995.

Under a clear signal, No. 56072 can be seen heading the 7C11 Onllwyn Washery to Abethaw towards Neath & Brecon Junction. The train is leaving the former Neath & Brecon Railway route, opened as far as Onllwyn in 1863, and Brecon in 1867, as it heads for Swansea Burrows Sidings for running round. This image makes for an interesting comparison with the earlier view of a Cwmgwrach departure, taken four years earlier. Note the development work that had already swept away the small engineering premises. 25 February 1998.

Winding up the Dulais Valley, No. 56092 heads an empty MGR past Cefn Coed just after midday, en route to Onllwyn. At the time landscaping work was taking place on the site of the former colliery of the same name, itself in production from 1930 to 1968. Cefn Coed Colliery Museum has seen the headgear and some surface buildings survive into the twenty-first century, unlike the now-scrapped No. 56092 – a 1981 product of Doncaster Works. 22 September 1998.

Continuing north along former Neath & Brecon Railway metals, we see No. 60063 heading between Crynant and Seven Sisters with the 6C11 empty MGR for Onllwyn Washery. The train loco emerged from Brush, Loughborough, in June 1991 and happily survives under DB ownership. 10 March 1997.

On a beautifully sunny evening in July 1996, No. 37796 backs the 6B75 empty MGR into the Onllwyn Washery complex. Opened in 1932, the washery was built to handle coal from local drift mines. Having undergone considerable alteration in both 1950 and 1993, the site was (and still is at the time of writing) receiving opencast mined coal by road from several locations. In 2007, 900,000 tons of coal were handled by the plant, half of which originated from the Selar opencast mine located just south of Glynneath. 17 July 1996.

Following on from the previous view, a member of the traincrew looks on as two mechanical shovels begin loading what will become the 7B75 20.40 Onllwyn Washery to Swansea Burrows Sidings. Of note to the left of the loco is the rake of 'internal user' former HUO hopper wagons, used for the movement and storage of coal around the washery site. With a 3.5-ton increase in capacity over the then standard 21-ton type, the HUOs were introduced in 1954 with bulk coal flows in mind, such as those to power stations. The advent of the HAA merry-go-round hoppers from the middle of the following decade saw the type cascaded to other flows, such as the conveyance of coke. 17 July 1996.

The 7B75 20.40 Onllwyn to Burrows, this time formed of PFA wagons and coal containers and hauled by No. 56052, awaits processing in the washery complex. The line beyond Onllwyn to Coelbren Junction, Brecon and Talyllyn Junction was closed by 1969. The rugged countryside evident in the background of this view gives a clue to the fact that part of the closed section, near Penwyllt, was used for its likeness to South Africa during the filming of the armoured train sequence in the 1972 film *Young Winston*, where the 1899 Boer ambush of a British Army train was re-enacted. In contrast to the preserved ex-GWR 0-4-2 No. 1466 – suitably disguised for its film role – No. 56052 was scrapped in 2009 after a life of just over twenty years. 13 October 1994.

The 1B96 10.55 Cardiff to Fishguard Harbour, hauled by No. 37425, skirts the River Loughor south of Llangennech on a misty day in August 2003, having swung south from the Swansea District Line at Morlais Junction. Looking at his map, the Author was convinced there would be a vantage point at or near this location from which to record a fine riverside view. However, the reality fell somewhat short of my expectations, though this hurried photo, taken from a tree next to a foot crossing, still merits inclusion – if only due to the subject matter! 12 August 2003.

Now we head inland from the previous shot. It was just as well Midsummer's Day was chosen to record No. 37895 hauling the 6Z60 13.45 Swansea Burrows to Gwaun-cae-Gurwen (GCG), as it was to be 19.45 before the train made it into this view at Pantyffynnon. Thanks to kind permission from the relief at the signal box of the same name, a relatively shadow-free lineside view – considering the late hour – was possible to record the train about to take the GCG Branch, having gained the Central Wales Line at Morlais, and Hendy Junction. 21 June 1995.

Turning 180 degrees from the previous view, and using the fine lower quadrant bracket guarding the northbound approach to Pantyffynnon as a frame, No. 37701 is seen beginning its journey to Swansea Burrows Sidings, having just left the GCG Branch with a load of washed coal. Again, kind permission from the Pantyffynnon signalman enabled this shot to be taken, once suitably attired with an orange tabard! The train is about to take part of the southern section of the Central Wales Line – often referred to as the 'Heart of Wales Line' – as part of its onward route. The Central Wales Line was completed to Craven Arms by 1868 by a number of different companies, all backed by the LNWR. 13 October 1994.

Crossing the River Amman between Pontamman and Ammanford, the loaded train seen in the previous view heads down the GCG Branch towards Pantyffynnon. Though not recorded at the time, No. 37701's train of gleaming anthracite is most likely the 6Z46 11.50 GCG Washery to Burrows Sidings, running slightly late. As will be seen, the Author was able to record No. 37701's empty and loaded workings on this fine October day, thanks in no small part to a tip-off from a friend that it was running. 13 October 1994.

With the ascent of the Amman Valley behind it, No. 37701 nears the end of its journey to GCG Washery and Disposal Point with what the Author believes is the 6Z45 08.45 from Burrows Sidings. The railway routes radiating east from Pantyffynnon, of which the GCG Branch was (at the time of writing) the sole survivor, evolved from the 1840s to the 1920s when the Abernant Branch was completed, the former junction to which is roughly where the end of the train is. 13 October 1994.

The 1 in 40 gradient on the approach to the exchange sidings at GCG is evident in this view of No. 37701 moving its train onwards from the previous shot towards the final destination. The train is in the process of crossing the A474 road, just visible below the fifth wagon. On a personal note, the car in which the Author made most of his journeys into South Wales during much of the period covered by this book – a 1984 Ford Orion GL – is to the left of the ground frame. 13 October 1994.

Returning to Midsummer's Day 1995; in just over twenty-five minutes No. 37895 has lifted its empty 6Z60 PFA consist from Pantyffynnon to the exchange sidings at GCG. The area has had a long association with coal mining, with up to seven pits in production by the early 1920s. The inevitable decline in this industry had, by the date of this view, left just the washery/disposal point in operation, taking output from local opencast workings. After a considerable period out of use, railborne traffic had returned to GCG at the time of writing, with Celtic Energy using the loading pad to dispatch coal from its opencast East Pit working. 21 June 1995.

With the traincrew in the process of running round the late-running 13.45 Burrows Sidings to GCG, No. 37895 catches some late evening sunshine at the head of the washery/disposal point sidings. Totally unscripted, a local boy had turned up to witness proceedings, during which he made known his displeasure at the noise emanating from the Class 37/7 by putting his fingers in his ears! 21 June 1995.

Revisiting the cloudless day of 13 October 1994 we see No. 37701 in the GCG exchange sidings, having swapped its rake of empty HEA hoppers for a corresponding rake filled with processed high-quality Welsh anthracite. A member of the traincrew looks on at what is most likely the late-running 6Z46 11.50 GCG to Burrows Sidings (with reference to the 'Section PE' working timetable of the period). 13 October 1994.

Travelling up the Heart of Wales Line, the southern end of Sugar Loaf Tunnel is the location for this view of a diverted Margam to Llanwern steel coil train. With a gradient of up to 1 in 60 on the approach to this scene, and with leading No. 37401 doing all the work over an ailing No. 37426, it is not too difficult to imagine how memorable the train's approach was! Having gone in and out several times as the thunderous roar got nearer, it can be seen that the sun made a timely appearance – much to the delight of all gathered! New to Darnall as D6968 in 1965, the lead loco moved to Canton as No. 37268 in 1977, with refurbishment and a move to Scotland in the mid-1980s. Happily, No. 37401 is still in service with DRS at the time of writing. 28 May 2000.

Though definitely more 'Mid' than 'South' Wales, the reason or excuse for showing a view near the northern end of Llangynllo Tunnel is that the subject, the 6Z83 14.50 Llanwern to Margam empty coil, originated and finished in South Wales. The beauty of the landscape through which much of the Heart of Wales Line runs is apparent in a scene where, on this occasion, Nos 37174 and 37375 made their presence known for many minutes before they appeared as they tackled the gradient to the tunnel, the southern portal of which marks the highest point of the line at 980 feet above sea level. Alas, both locomotives were scrapped in 2008. 28 May 2000.

The main line approach to Llanelli is the location for this view of No. 37894 hauling a uniform rake of Mainline-liveried MEA wagons en route to Coedbach Washery, near Kidwelly, for loading. Dominating the background is the Trostre Tinplate Works, a site which began production under the ownership of the Steel Company of Wales in 1951. The area's expertise in tinplate production, together with a high level of post-war unemployment in the Llanelli area, were the key factors in the location of the plant which, in subsequent years, passed through British Steel and Corus ownership. At the time of writing Tata Steel employs 700 people on the site. 8 May 1996.

The extensive regeneration of the coastline just to the west of Llanelli is apparent in this view of Nos 47815 and 47847 top and tailing a Cardiff-bound rugby special. Alas, the Author's records of the day are incomplete; however, the train is most likely the 10.12 from Carmarthen – run in connection with the match between Wales and Ireland at the Cardiff Millennium Stadium. The area to the right of the train would have previously been dominated by Llanelli Steelworks. Opened in 1907 by the Llanelly Steel Company, the works passed into Duport Steel ownership in 1960. Closure came in 1981, when Duport went bankrupt. 19 March 2005.

In contrast to the style this book has taken thus far in respect of starting coverage of a branch line where it commences, in the case of the former Burry Port and Gwendraeth line to Cwm-mawr we start at the end of the line. The main reason for this is that all the images shown of this unique route were taken on the final day of service prior to closure three days later, so it was considered fitting to follow the train down the line. Here, No. 08994 awaits the formation of its train at Cwm-mawr Disposal Point. 29 March 1996.

With the final lorry having delivered its load of opencast-mined anthracite, a mechanical shovel pushes the remains into the loading hopper for the disposal point. The coal was destined for the Coedbach Washery at the foot of the branch. Kind permission was given for the Author and others to enter the site to record this rather sad occasion. 29 March 1996.

Staff members at the Cwm-mawr Disposal Point pose for a photograph next to the cab of the lorry that had delivered the final coal. Though relatively small by the standards of similar sites still extant at the time it seemed odd that, while local opencast mining was still taking place, the disposal point was to close for good. Unfortunately, the site and line passed into history three days later, on 1 April 1996. 29 March 1996.

Looking down the Gwendreath Valley from the disposal point, No. 08994 is seen at the head of its formed up train of HEA hoppers. Cwm-mawr was the end point of the only surviving part of a small network of lines built by the Burry Port & Gwendraeth Railway (BP&GR). This company evolved from various schemes to link collieries and limestone pits to the sea at Kidwelly. Chief among the earlier undertakings was the Kidwelly & Llanelly Canal, authorised in 1812, the course of which was used by BP&GR for the line to Cwm-mawr, resulting in clearance issues that required cut-down locomotives and rolling stock – the latter where necessary. 29 March 1996.

Moving to the other end of No. 08994's train, we see the traincrew for the final departure pose for the handful of photographers present. One wonders how many years of railway experience these fine gentlemen had between them by the date of this photo. Later in the day, however, it may well have been a new experience for them to be gestured to stop, and wait for the sun to come out, for the same photographers, as the train approached Pontyberem. The fact that these generous men obliged is evidenced on the cover of this book! 29 March 1996.

The fact that this was the last working from Cwm-mawr, with a possible resultant increase in lorry traffic, was not lost on many of the local population – a few of whom turned out to briefly hold up the train to make their feelings known, as can be seen at the road crossing in the village of Pontyates. At its inception the line was laid out on the towpath of the canal it superseded, with deviations into the drained canal course itself being necessary to pass under bridges. This resulted in short downgrades on the route, which was finally opened to Cwm-mawr in 1886. 29 March 1996.

The final working from Cwm-mawr nears the end of its run down the Gwendraeth Valley as it passes Trimsaran behind No. 08994. The train is nearing the point at which a line diverged to serve Burry Port, via Pembrey. This line, often prone to flooding, was the chief reason that diesel-mechanical Class 03 locomotives with cut-down cabs were used on the BP&GR system in later years – often in threes to take account of the stiff gradients. The Burry Port section's demise in 1984, together with the corresponding reopening of the link to Kidwelly Junction, allowed the use of more powerful cut down Class 08s, where flood water was not such an issue with the type's electric transmission. 29 March 1996.

The sand dunes bordering the waters of the Bae Caerfyrddin at St Ishmael, between Ferryside and Kidwelly, sees No. 37402 briefly disturb the peace with the 1R38 13.35 Fishguard to Rhymney. With a striking backdrop to a colourful train, the view perhaps provides a fitting finale to this collection, with its combination of classic traction and fine Welsh scenery. Happily, this beautiful and important stretch of railway remains for future generations. As for No. 37402 (new to Canton in April 1965 as D6974), moves to Landore and Laira, renumbering to 37274 and a transfer to Scotland after completion of its 1985 refurbishment were followed by further travels and eventual service with DRS, with whom it remains at the time of writing. A fitting tribute to a locomotive type that will inexorably be linked with South Wales. 31 August 2004.

Also available from Amberley Publishing

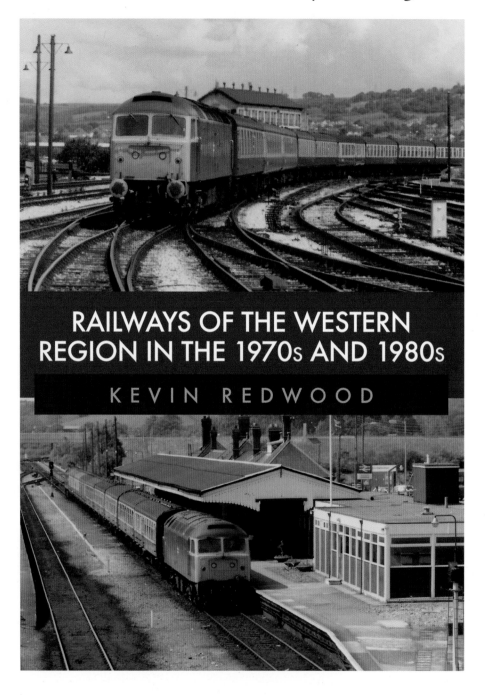

RAILWAYS OF THE WESTERN
REGION IN THE 1970s AND 1980s

KEVIN REDWOOD

Available from all good bookshops or to order direct
Please call **01453-847-800**
www.amberley-books.com